Dissection

poems by

Nikki Thompson

Finishing Line Press
Georgetown, Kentucky

Dissection

Copyright © 2016 by Nikki Thompson
ISBN 978-1-944251-62-8 First Edition
All rights reserved under International and Pan-American Copyright Conventions.
No part of this book may be reproduced in any manner whatsoever without written permission from the publisher, except in the case of brief quotations embodied in critical articles and reviews.

ACKNOWLEDGMENTS

Cobalt Review: "Panic," "Speech Therapy," "Getting a Ride"
Mason's Road: "Roller Coaster," "Bathing"
Palimpsest: A Creative Journal of the Humanities: "Losing Distance"
spork: "$f(x)=2x+1$," "$12 + 13 + 14 + \ldots$," "$a, ar, ar^2, ar^3\ldots$," "$y'=3-2x$," "$\lim_{n\to\infty} \underline{ar}^n = 0, \underline{}_{1-r}$"

"Onomatopoeia," "Translation" and "Pitter Patter" written for Henry Hung and the Klaxton Mutant Allstars

I would like to thank Teresa Walsh, Kate Godfrey, and Jen Siraganian for all the years of writing support and caffeine. Thank you to past writing groups and professors: Opal Palmer Adisa, Rae Armantrout, Kathy Barr, Hugh Behm-Steinberg, Rebekah Bloyd, Kate Godfrey, John Laskey, Karen Salinger, and Ann Williams, and most especially Judith Serin and Betsy Davids. Special thanks to my husband, Edwin Maguire, for being so supportive of my poetry and art.

Editor: Christen Kincaid

Cover Art: Edwin Maguire

Author Photo: Edwin Maguire

Cover Design: Elizabeth Maines

Printed in the USA on acid-free paper.
Order online: www.finishinglinepress.com
  also available on amazon.com

Author inquiries and mail orders:
Finishing Line Press
P. O. Box 1626
Georgetown, Kentucky 40324
U. S. A.

Table of Contents

INTEGRATING INTO DIFFERENTIATION: Prose Poems

$f(x)=2x+1$	1
$12 + 13 + 14 + \ldots$	2
$a, ar, ar^2, ar^3\ldots$	3
$y'=3-2x$	4
$\lim_{n\to\infty} \dfrac{ar^n}{1-r} = 0$	5

SESTINAS

Losing Distance	8
Pu-erh	10

RHYTHM: Jazz Poems

Onomatopoeia	14
Translation	15
Pitter Patter	16

DISSECTION: Prose Poems

Panic	18
A Respite	19
Speech Therapy	20
Blood in Three Parts	21
Normalcy	23
Roller Coaster	25
Bathing	26
Getting a Ride	27
Electric Can Opener	28
Breathe	29

To my parents

INTEGRATING INTO DIFFERENTIATION:
Prose Poems

$f(x)=2x+1$

I'm crushed by the paranoia fed to me in utero, as deep as my DNA. An assigned value—in this case systematic second-guessing—determines the dependent variable's corresponding value, and I can't walk out the door without checking the stove and then returning to check again. I resent considering potential disasters and unforeseeable consequences until I'm paralyzed. Pre-determined flight, real world obligations—these equations teach me to trust myself. Still the dependent variable is the function of the independent variable, so my mom calls every Sunday to make sure I'm taking my vitamins, not walking alone at night, still breathing.

12 + 13 + 14 + ...

I'm falling apart at the edges. Thread by thread I unravel—each promise made, each commitment. I secure one strand, another loosens, I never finish the first. The series diverges and my ends won't weave back together—the fringes widening, the intact center shrinking. Like painting an over eight mile bridge, I'm back at the beginning before I get to the end. With fingers cramped into permanent fists, I'm left to increasing terms that extend into namelessness.

a, ar, ar², ar³…

I arrange a contrast between me and the wall, waiting for no one to ask me to dance. Beyond junior high it's called mingling and career advancement, so the dancing has been eliminated. In a progression the terms are different, but the relationship is the same. I intrude on readings, openings, parties and try to attach myself to the clumped conversations. I watch for arrows—a glance or gesture of inclusion. Secretly I don't want to force my brain into the horrors of small talk and going nowhere.

I avoid the food table, frightened by the predatory lunges for cheese and chocolate-covered strawberries. I'd rather settle into the familiar exchanges of four or five friends. Even if the terms are consecutive and I'm supposed to learn from the past, I'm still trying to think of what to say. I edge into a group of minglers, like a tight parallel parking job. Always the last to know, I realize I've spoken aloud and my brain has betrayed me with a witticism. Are they rolling their eyes in laughter or pity?

y'=3−2x

I'm left grasping after calendar pages. What I thought was months away is long over. Just as a function changes value at a certain rate, I'm behind again and never was caught up and more keeps piling on. The function's value depends on the variable.

I wish for an eight day week and then have to remind myself that I would only commit to more and be left wishing for a nine day week. The rate of the changing function is consistently fickle, technically derivative. Time is not the problem, rather it's not understanding when too much is too much until I'm either immobile or shrieking.

$$\lim_{n \to \infty} \frac{ar^n}{1-r} = 0$$

Daily I wait in line, forced to fade away, as one after another I'm shuffled to the end. My diminishing space goes unacknowledged and continues to be invaded—the terms are getting smaller as the value approaches infinite. I imagine shoving back, even if it is the wrong solution. I consult the pinball—ping!—and am left careening around corners and ricocheting off ringers. The inconsideration and self-absorption is nibbling at my tolerance, eating its way toward my limits, and I explode to infinite.

SESTINAS

Losing Distance

We stand tall at the beginning of loss
Too long the weeks leading to ending
Bitter and absent, the reminder of your toothbrush
Your breath before sleeping—fragrant with whiskey
I cry and rant at distance
While accepting another unfulfilled need

You never saw my needs
Claiming they were absent, at a loss
You used the excuse of distance
And familial obligation as a reason for ending
Each meandering hour with a whiskey
Kiss, leaving instead a toothbrush

To establish your presence, your territorial toothbrush
To claim your possession and need
Of me. The sudden sting of whiskey
Coating nose and throat with peat and loss
As every beginning makes its way to ending
And each connection stretches into distance

I see the patterns and swan dive into distance
Throwing out your toothbrush
Demanding an ending
Realizing your offerings are not my needs
And you will let others choose, so you can remain lost
Clinging to memories of each previous bottle of whiskey

Days afterward I drink the last shot of whiskey
Alone and glad for the distance
Wondering when I will feel the loss
And throwing out traces of you: first the toothbrush
Then the petty transgressions and slights you needed
Followed by the maybe endings

But each ending is a new ending
Each beginning more faded and whiskey-
Stained until the realization of our needs
Is the realization of unconscionable distances
Our relationship nothing more than a two-year brush
With half-hearted devotion, so we resign ourselves to loss

And embrace ending, stretching the distance
With a swallow of whiskey and a discarded toothbrush
Until our needs no longer remember the emptiness of loss.

Pu-erh

Look how soon this becomes a pattern.
We travel a path slender like a needle,
As much a routine as the smell of bacon
And the shrieking kettle announcing tea.
Even so the routines of relationship become tentative
When we hide from the fears and hopes of intimacy's cavern.

We hesitantly poke our heads into fear's cavern,
Looking for answers and future's fortunes in patterns
Of darkness and the unknown. Our responses tentative,
Narrow as the shaft of a needle,
Ephemeral as the steam wavering from a tea
Cup without the conviction of hissing, snapping bacon.

Through the wafting stench of home cooking and bacon
We trudge hour after hour through these ambiguous caverns
Wishing for the calm of tea,
But knowing that the violence of puncturing is a pattern
Sewn through the decades by generations of needles.
If we want strength we must endure the tentative.

With a now full of unknown and tentative
We must be careful not to burn the bacon
Or lose the needle
As we make our way through this new cavern
And assign ourselves a lifelong pattern
Of getting old and sipping tea.

Alongside the metamorphosis of steeping tea
We talk and figure and speculate on tentative
Assumptions, needing to clarify so as to create the pattern
And find the recipes that call for bacon
As we explore the secrets of our caverns
And puncture our uncertainties and conditionalities with needles.

The rents that happen, we will mend with needles
And mismatched fabrics. We will drink tea
To aid the healing and fill the caverns
With a promise less tentative
Than the conflict of flesh and fat in cooking bacon
When determining the future's enduring pattern.

Each generation's needles return to sewing the tentative
Traditions of tea-taking and curing bacon
Within the walls of intimacy's caverns and the relationship of
     patterns.

RHYTHM:
Jazz Poems

Onomatopoeia

Peeking pensive pounding
the duopoint of horns
the undertone of rattling

Swerving slingshot swaying
the ping of piano keys
the trill of a trumpet

Piercing cry chaos
Frantic fierce
Stop

Calmer now
Ending now
End

Translation

I listen to the
rhythm of chaos
the music into language

I tiptoe into
words and horns and pianos
sliding, slippery

I sway
so no one can see
right can't keep up with left

I feel the drag
pulling, pounding, curving
then clanking, clanging, wailing

Creeping towards silence

Pitter Patter

dance and swoop
along the sound line
pattern of footsteps

rain falling into water
concentric circles
outward to nothingness

slide of horns, pause
the emotion tentative
questioning then certain

rhythm followed by
chaos and cacophony
back to rhythm

swooping to irrevocable

DISSECTION:
Prose Poems

My carotid artery dissected, and I had a stroke when I was 31.

Panic

I said, Dad, you have to come get me; he said I had to get an ambulance—he was 400 miles away. In my head, I was calm. It had taken so long to figure how the phone worked, to figure out Dad started with a D, to figure out Send.

I said I didn't need an ambulance; Grace said she would drive. The two of us hobbled down the stairs to her car—Grace at my right side, completely numb.

Months later, Grace said she had seen the MRI of my brain—all gray with a white gash in the middle. While we waited, I kept saying how strange it all was to be the one lying in the hospital bed. The doctors kept coming by and saying I would have a room soon. A crazy lady was yelling in the bed next to mine, hospital attendants were apologizing. Finally, they took me upstairs. The orderlies wheeled me lying down. The walls were too low; the ceiling too high. Imagining I looked calm, I was out of control, panicked. In my room, Grace fell asleep on the little pull-out couch. Driving from San Diego to San Francisco, my brother got to the hospital at three in the morning.

One doctor with huge pearl earrings said I was so young, it was so strange. They found it mentioned only a few times in the literature. My carotid artery had dissected; I'd had a stroke.

A Respite

They took me in an ambulance from Kaiser San Francisco to Kaiser Vallejo; they said it was the best place to recover. The paramedics strapped me to a bed. Too far above the ground, with a paramedic next to me, I was nervous, but I saw green and orange and yellow and purple speeding by. My mom was in the front, talking to the ambulance driver—two disembodied voices.

Before ... too much. A million things to call my responsibility, to pull my attention this way and that. The lists kept getting longer. I couldn't say no. And more people kept asking me; I kept asking myself. Followed by ... crash.

Then ... calm. I couldn't recall what I was supposed to do. My world was slow. Physical therapy—walking between bars and a therapist stretching my arm; speech therapy—worksheets like I was in school again; and then lunch. Occupational therapy—cooking and electricity to make my hand extend; more physical therapy—how to get in the car and how to crawl on the floor if I fell, and then to my room. Visits from friends: the flowers, the gifts, the cards, the love. So many people; they flew up from LA, rented cars in San Francisco. Outside on the patio, I sat with big groups of friends, eating the lunches they had brought me. On the sun-covered deck, I had long conversations with my fellow patients and short ones passing in the hallways.

Paused, I was content.

Speech Therapy

Hair cut at ten, accountant at two, and I felt so strange. Four days of headache gone, but I couldn't move properly. I would be fine. When I opened my mouth to cancel the appointments, slowly, slowly, the sentences dripped off my tongue. I would be fine.

Days later, when I was at Kaiser Vallejo, talking slowly, like I was Southern my mom said, I wheeled to the speech therapist. The room was small, made even smaller by partitioning. The speech therapist had her desk by the door. I could barely fit my wheelchair in. Would I be fine? She beat a pencil and said a two-syllable word—baby—matching the word to the beat. Then she told me to try. I did. Ba-by. Baby. Would I be fine?

Blood in Three Parts

I.
"I have to take your blood." Waking up, sleepily, I would joke with him—about what I can't remember. I couldn't turn in bed, my right side with a pillow underneath—I could only offer my arm. Inside the curtain surrounding my bed, he had to measure how fast I could make a blood clot—lower than two, too low; higher than three, too high. With three other women and the curtains closed, before the morning blood-draw, I was alone in the still room of night.

II.
I left the hospital with a binder (my medical record, a brochure on sex after a stroke, and exercises), two kinds of pills, and instructions to get a blood test and watch a video on blood thinner. My dad took me to Kaiser Sunset that first time, because I couldn't drive anymore. Beige and gray buildings, hospital neutral, sprawled along Sunset; one building where I had my blood drawn, another for the neurologist, another where we parked. We made our way through overpasses between buildings, floors, hallways, elevators, and back to the ground floor, to the office where I would watch the video. In one scene an older woman, dressed like one of the actresses from The Golden Girls, said "I like to prepare healthy food for my husband, but we have to watch leafy greens, because of Vitamin K." I remember thinking, I'm not old like this woman, but at least I don't have to eat hospital food anymore.

III.
My dad drove me once a week to Kaiser Woodland Hills to get my blood drawn. He with his slouching walk, I with my cane. The two of us would weave our way past the construction toward the blood draw waiting room. I would wait for one woman, who only left a small bruise, letting others go ahead of me. The room was a pink color, like drawings of organs in a medical textbook. I sat on one side of a row of booths and chairs, the phlebotomist sat on the other. I gave her my arm. Then my other arm. Then sometimes my wrist. I looked intently at the cartoons and pictures of dogs in the cubicle and away from small bags of blood she was taking out of my body.

Normalcy

I.

We would sit out on the deck, chatting, enjoying the sun, not thinking about the difficulty of getting through the door. We were too new to a wheelchair, so we would watch as someone would try to cross the threshold, pushing fast enough to get over the hump. If one of us failed, the door would close against the wheelchair, front wheels inside, back wheels outside, until a passerby took pity. Embarrassing, but what could we do?

II.

Trying to navigate the world outside the hospital, I noticed the pavement under the wheelchair, not the hospital's smooth floors, but the bump, bump, bump of the yellow safety strip into the hotel lobby. I was almost ready to go home the hospital staff said, so I was allowed to go to the hotel where my parents were staying. I was thankful it was night: rolling through the lobby without being noticed.

Now, I was in LA at my parents' house. My family folded my wheelchair up and put it in the car, and we drove to the beach. It felt strange to be pushed and sitting: the crunch, crunch of wheels running over sand on pavement. The perspective was different; the horizon lower, the sky more expansive. I had to depend on whoever could push my chair. No one I knew would see, unlike at my parents' house when the neighbors would stop by and ask how I was doing.

III.
I was almost out of the hospital, so I went to lunch with my parents. I used my four point cane and was scared. My old world had become unfamiliar; the safe world had become the hospital. People would stare at me, I thought: the disparity of a young person acting like an old person.

In therapy I went from a four-point cane to a one-point cane. I was making progress, they told me. Then I was ready to walk without a cane. I was ecstatic; I was on my way towards normalcy. But now, back in San Francisco, I sometimes think of my cane sitting in my parents' garage. I think how I could use my cane as concealment or protection, especially on a crowded bus.

Roller Coaster

One of the first nights at my parent's house, we decided to go for a walk—all four of us and the two dogs. Since I couldn't climb the hill, I left my four-point cane and took the wheelchair. Even that tired me out. Like walking, I moved my feet back and forth, back and forth, careful not to get them stuck under the chair. I gripped the wheels with my hands, pushed, and then let go; gripped again, pushed, and let go; over and over. I wasn't used to walking with my hands.

My dad wondered if the dogs could pull me. So we strapped their leashes over the handles of my wheelchair. Billie, my Boxer-Pitbull mix, put her head down and pulled, like she was born to it. Roxy, my brother's Doberman-Rottweiler mix, rolled her eyes and kept trying to escape.

As the dogs were dragging me down the hill, I was on a roller coaster. My family was all here beside me, and we were laughing, and no one was bickering, and I was one part of a whole.

Bathing

I could bathe myself now, but I couldn't wash my hair, even with the detachable showerhead. My arm wouldn't reach above my head. I sat on the hard white plastic chair with the holes. My mom and I talked, just like we had for years. That felt comfortable. My mom bathing me though, that was not comfortable.

At least here was the bathroom I grew up in, not the hospital bathroom. I had to be showered by the nurse. She wrapped me in a big towel and wheeled me across the room, in front of my three roommates and whoever else happened by. In physical therapy, they showed me how to use the hard white chair that my dad bought at Home Depot. They had a special tub set up just for that purpose.

I felt old, older than my mom. She had to bathe me again.

Getting a Ride

Being 31, I felt fifteen again. I had to ask my parents for a ride to a friend's, to the museum, to the movies. I was 400 miles from home, where I would ride my bike to the grocery store, to the cleaners, to the shops on Valencia Street. My old life was gone. In LA the distances were enormous—The Valley to Los Feliz, to downtown LA, to the West Side. Then a ride home with a friend. I was grateful, but in high school again: waiting, impatient, silently raging, until I turned sixteen.

With my physical therapist, I wheeled out to my mom's car in the parking lot. She did the transfer first, showing me how to place my hands and not bump my head against the window. Then I tried. She said my dad's truck would be easier. Now, I always had to sit in the front seat with my four-point, then my one-point, cane. My friend Jesse's car was low to the ground, and I fell into the seat when I got in. He said that his grandma had the same problem.

Electric Can Opener

Now I knew why you would want an electric can opener. I used to think: only the old and frail can stand the hum going round and round.

Beyond the sink the electric can opener looms large. But in the drawer the hand can opener rests quietly alongside tea balls, cheese slicers, cookie cutters. A hand grasps the can opener, feeling the rubber handles and the metal underneath. The opener is clipped to the side of a can, jaws deftly fit with circular blade on top and teeth on the bottom. The smoothness of the turn, turn, turn, and voila! the can is open.

Now I longed to hear the magnet snapped to the can and that whir, whir, whir. I was not strong enough to use a hand can opener anymore. I was only 31, but I knew what it was like to feel old and frail.

Breathe

I stretched into the Bow Asana, gripped my ankles, raised my knees, my thighs, trying, but couldn't lift off the ground. Imagining how my body used to be, before the stroke, my thighs and upper body would reach for the sky, my back would curve into an arch—how right the stretch felt.

Yoga was acceptance, and I did tolerate my body's limitations, mostly. I endured my wonky balance and my right arm wobble, while stretching my arms and legs outward in Warrior II. To get from an upside down "V" to my chest thrust upward, front knee bent, leg back, I had to grab my ankle like a beginner, instead of smoothly moving my leg forward. What I couldn't accept was my breathing. If I was in my car, driving, I thought of my breath's shallowness. During yoga I thought of the three part breath—belly, diaphragm, chest—the most basic breath. I used to be able to breathe with the pose; inhale, arch, exhale, fold. Now, when did I breathe in, breathe out? The teacher said, but I lost it.

I saw the changes; I accepted the changes, almost.

Nikki Thompson is a poet, book artist (aka Deconstructed Artichoke Press), and happily failed architect. She fled Southern California for UC Berkeley, where she earned a degree in architecture and edited *Berkeley Fiction Review*. She remained in the Bay Area and earned her MFA in creative writing from California College of the Arts in 2002. Her work has appeared in *Mason's Road, Cobalt Review* and *Eleven Eleven,* among others. She is a runner-up for the Earl Weaver Baseball Writing Prize and a nominee for a Pushcart Prize. She currently resides in Sacramento, California, with her husband and daughter. Her website is www.deconstructedartichokepress.com.